YOUNG GEOGRAPHER

FOOD
AND
FARMING

SUSAN REED-KING

Wayland

Young Geographer

The Changing Earth
Food and Farming
Journeys
Natural Resources
Protecting the Planet
Settlements
The World's Population
The World's Weather

Editor: Kate Asser
Designer: Mark Whitchurch
Consultant: Dr Tony Binns, geography lecturer at Sussex University

Front cover picture: People gathering rice in Sumatra, Indonesia.
Frontispiece: A simple ox-driven irrigation system in Ethiopia.
Back cover picture: Newly-harvested pumpkins in New Hampshire, USA.

First published in 1992 by
Wayland (Publishers) Ltd
61 Western Road, Hove
East Sussex BN3 1JD, England

© Copyright 1992 Wayland (Publishers) Ltd

British Library Cataloguing in Publication Data
Reed-King, Susan
Food and Farming. – (Young Geographer)
I. Title. II. Series
630

ISBN 0 7502 0440 0

Typeset by Type Study, Scarborough, England
Printed in Italy by Rotolito Lombarda S.p.A
Bound in France by A.G.M.

National Curriculum Attainment Targets

This book is most directly relevant to the following Attainment Targets in the Geography National Curriculum at Key Stage 2. The information can help in the following ways:

Attainment Target 2 (Knowledge and understanding of places) Comparing the features and occupations of a locality outside the local area with those of the local area; appreciating different types of land-use; understanding the impact of landscape, weather and wealth on a developing community.

Attainment Target 3 (Physical geography) Describing contrasting weather conditions in parts of the world.

Attainment Target 4 (Human geography) Understanding how settlements throughout the world differ in size; giving reasons for the way land is used; understanding the factors behind the growth and development of settlements.

Attainment Target 5 (Environmental geography) Studying how people have changed the environment; suggesting how the environment might be improved and pollution avoided; discussing whether some environments need special protection; investigating unintended effects of managing the environment.

Contents

Introduction	4
Food matters	6
Keeping livestock	8
Cereal crops	10
Fruit and vegetables	12
Luxury crops	14
Enough for all?	16
The environment	20
How healthy is your food?	24
Crops of the future	26
A changing world	28
Glossary	30
Books to read	31
Notes for activities	31
Index	32

All the words that are in **bold** appear in the glossary on page 30.

Introduction

We all need food to stay alive. Farmers produce this food. In the richer **industrial countries**, like Europe, Canada and the USA, farmers use the latest **technology** and farming methods. Only a small number of farmers are needed to produce food for the whole country. However, in much of Africa, India, Asia and South America, farmers do not have much machinery, so many more people are needed. In these places the climate and soil often cause farmers problems, and sometimes people can go hungry. The **population** of the world is also increasing in these areas, so that it is important for farmers to find ways to produce enough food.

Below: Combine harvesters cut and process grain efficiently and quickly.

Until about 10,000 years ago, everyone had to find food for themselves. People moved around hunting wild animals and picking wild fruit and grain. Scientists know, from remains that have been dug up, that people in the Middle East were the first to sow grains of wild wheat deliberately, instead of

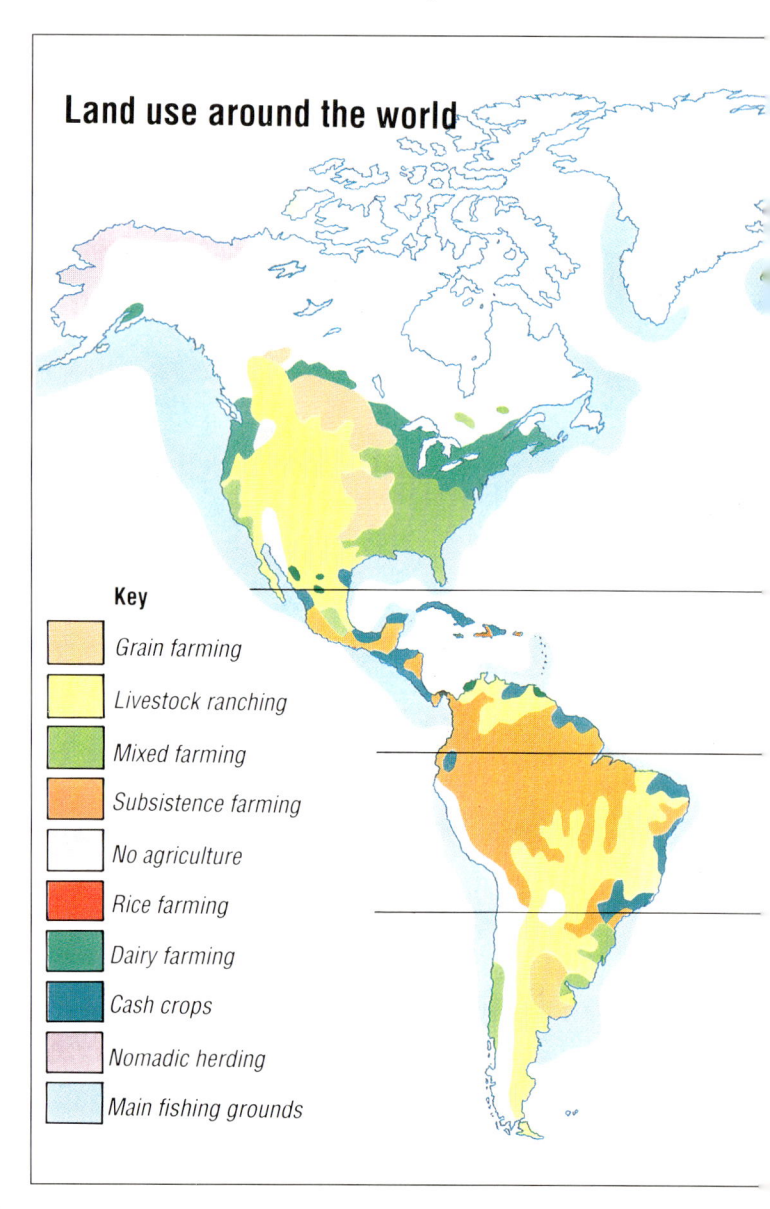

Land use around the world

Key
- Grain farming
- Livestock ranching
- Mixed farming
- Subsistence farming
- No agriculture
- Rice farming
- Dairy farming
- Cash crops
- Nomadic herding
- Main fishing grounds

depending on nature. A few hundred years later, people were keeping pigs in what is now Iraq, and were farming cattle in Greece.

Once people could grow crops and keep animals, they began to live together in farming settlements, like the one some 5,000 years ago at Sumer in Mesopotamia.

The Sumerians grew barley, wheat, apples, dates and grapes on the fertile land between the rivers Euphrates and Tigris (now in Iraq). They kept sheep and goats for meat and milk, and used oxen to plough the land. The Sumerians also used the two rivers to **irrigate** their farmland.

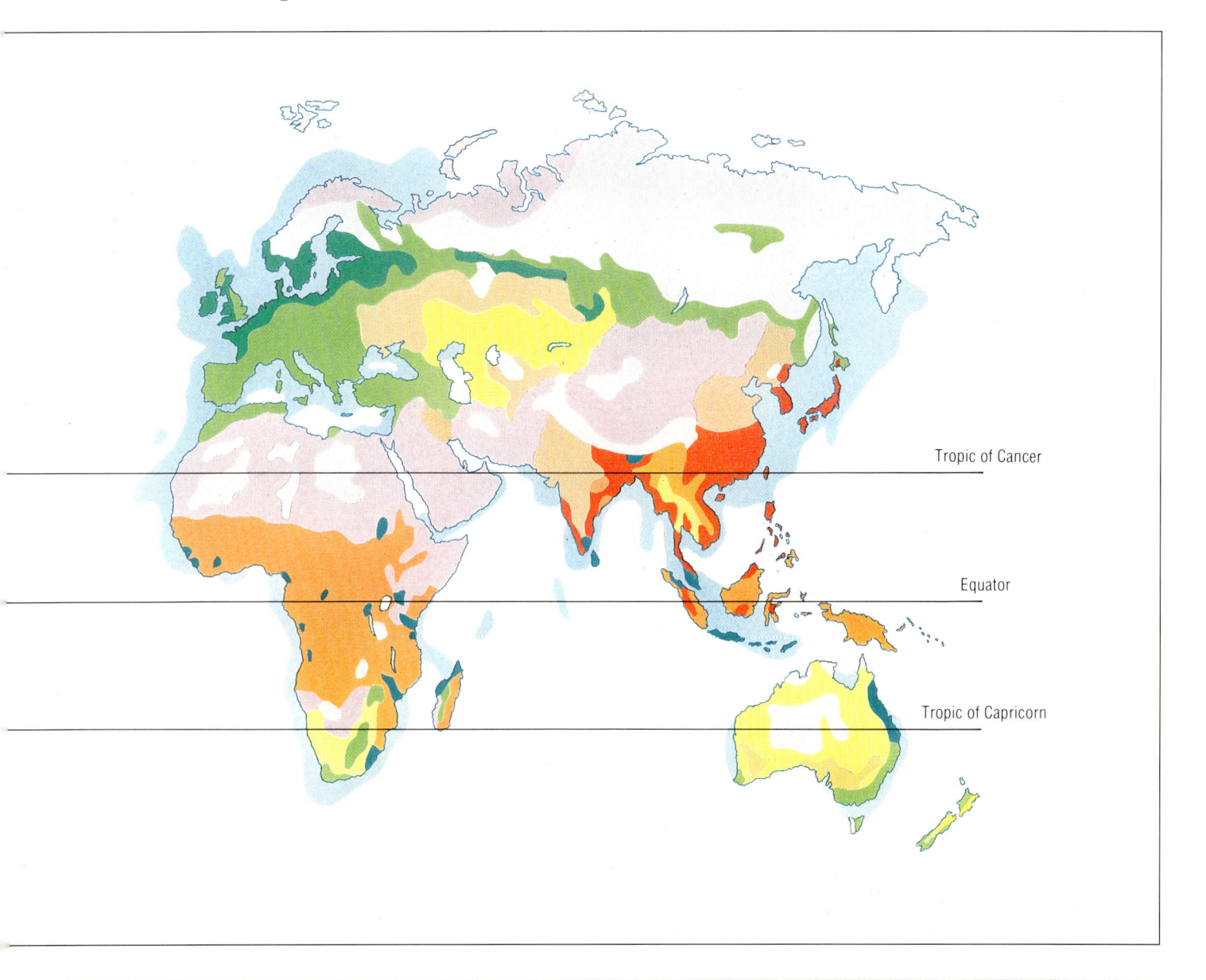

Food matters

If you want to be healthy and fit, you must eat a balanced diet of food which gives you energy and nourishment. Your body needs proteins which repair any damage to skin or bones, and also help you to grow. Meat, fish, cheese, nuts and pulses contain proteins. The carbohydrates found in starchy foods like bread, potatoes and rice give you energy. Vitamins fight off disease, so you should eat plenty of fresh fruit and vegetables, as well as dairy products and fish oils. Your body also needs fats from butter and oils to keep warm, and traces of minerals like iron to keep healthy. Iron comes from liver and spinach but also chocolate, which some people prefer!

The colourful foods displayed here not only look good – they are also good for your body.

Left: In large western-style supermarkets, customers can select fresh fruit from many countries.

Below: Locally-grown vegetables on sale in a mountain village market in Peru, South America.

Everyone needs a nourishing diet, but exactly what food people eat depends on where they live. Some kinds of crops and animals are suited to cooler climates and others to hotter places. In the past, people only ate the plants and animals that came from their own part of the world.

Over many centuries, certain foods have become the **staple diet** of a particular area. Wild rice comes from India but is now the main food eaten throughout India, China and South-east Asia. Potatoes and maize first came from South America but today they are also popular in many other places.

In western Europe, North America and Australia, people often shop in supermarkets. These sell food that comes from all over the world. In poorer countries, most people buy food at markets selling local produce. Some markets offer a wide range of foods but in parts of Africa and India, when crops fail, there may be little food available.

Keeping livestock

Farmers everywhere keep livestock for meat or dairy products. Industrial countries have many **intensive farms** with thousands of animals fed by machines, kept in a small space. These farms produce large amounts of food cheaply. In poorer countries however, farmers can only afford to keep a few animals for themselves.

Beef cattle are farmed in industrial countries, especially in North America and Australia, and in parts of South America and West Africa. Dairy cattle are kept mostly in northern Europe and New Zealand. India has more cattle per person than anywhere else, but they are working animals and are not kept for their meat.

On intensive farms, animals are often fed by machines. This method of farming produces cheap meat, but some people think that it is an unnatural way of keeping animals.

Ranches in rainforests

In richer countries people can afford to eat meat regularly. Beef products are so popular in these places that farmers in South and Central America have cleared vast areas of rainforest for cattle ranches.

Cattle need rich grass for grazing. However, rainforest soil is too poor to grow grass well. After a while, the soil becomes exhausted and more rainforest must be cleared. The farmers need money, but many people believe rainforests are better suited to a different type of farming.

Cattle in a burnt-out area of the Brazilian rainforest. The natural forest is behind.

Sheep and goats can adapt to many different climates. There are sheep in the Middle East, but also in mild New Zealand and cool northern Europe. Goats can survive on poor grazing and are popular for their milk and meat in **tropical regions**. In Arctic places, not many animals can survive the extreme cold, but people do farm reindeer. Reindeer originally grazed wild on the **tundra**, but the Lapp people have herded them for centuries.

Chickens first came from Asia, but their eggs and meat are now eaten all over the world. Pigs are farmed in northern Europe, especially in Denmark, and the western Soviet Republics.

These reindeer are in northern Norway. The animals are well-suited to Arctic winters, but their herders need modern skidoos to move around in snow.

9

Cereal crops

You may not give grass more than a passing thought, but without this plant family, livestock would have no grazing and people would have no cereal crops. Wheat, maize, rice, barley, millet, sorghum and oats are all grasses and provide the nourishing grains we call cereals.

The most widely-grown cereal is wheat. It is best suited to the **temperate regions** of the world, which offer a warm summer climate and regular rainfall. Normally wheat is sown in spring and harvested in summer, but in milder climates a type known as winter

Wheat, with its plump grains, is a popular cereal in many different countries from the North American prairies to the hotter parts of India.

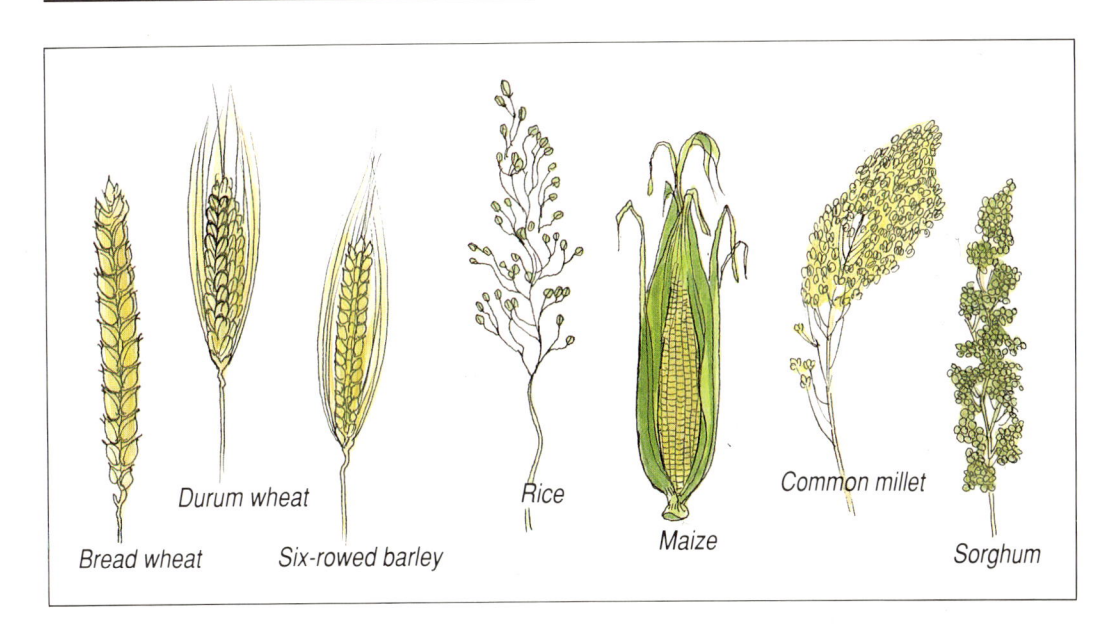

Left: *All these vital cereals belong to the grass family.*

Bread wheat, Durum wheat, Six-rowed barley, Rice, Maize, Common millet, Sorghum

Below: *In the Philippine Islands of South-east Asia, rice is grown in flooded, flat terraces, cut into steep mountainsides.*

wheat is also grown. Today there are thousands of wheat varieties but the most common are bread wheat and durum wheat, which is used to make pasta. The climate and large areas of suitable land in the Ukraine make this area the world's leading wheat producer, followed by China, the USA, India and Canada.

About half the world's population depends on one crop – rice. It is the staple food of millions of people in Asia. Rice needs to be grown in flooded fields, so it can easily be cultivated in the low-lying areas of China, India, Bangladesh, Japan and countries of South-east Asia.

Maize is now the world's second most widely-grown cereal. It originally came from Central America, but is now common in the temperate regions, as well as in hotter areas, like Africa.

Millet grows well in dry, poor soils and so is a valuable crop in parts of Africa and India. Its strong-tasting, small seeds are used to make flatbreads and porridges, and are also a useful animal feed. Sorghum is another important cereal in Africa and the Indian subcontinent.

Fruit and vegetables

The world's farmers grow a huge variety of fruit and vegetables. Each kind is suited to a particular climate, as the map opposite shows.

In temperate regions the hours of daylight and the temperature change with the seasons, although there is plenty of rain all year. Few plants will grow in the cold, dark winter, so most crops are sown in spring, when the temperature rises and there is more daylight. Root crops like potatoes, carrots, beets and turnips, as well as onions and cabbages, are grown everywhere from northern Europe to northern India.

Temperate fruits usually grow on deciduous trees or bushes, which shed their leaves to survive the winter cold. Apples, pears, cherries, raspberries and currants grow well in cooler temperate areas, but peaches, apricots, grapes, peppers and oranges need plenty of sunshine to ripen. They are grown in Mediterranean countries, California and north and southern Africa, where frosts rarely harm the fruit.

In hotter, drier areas, like much of Africa, the Middle East and India, irrigation schemes are often needed to help farmers grow crops. Many kinds of beans, peas and ground nuts are grown in this hot climate, as are aubergines, peppers, tomatoes, melons and dates.

Harvesting cranberries. These small, sharp berries are grown in boggy areas in the north-east of the USA.

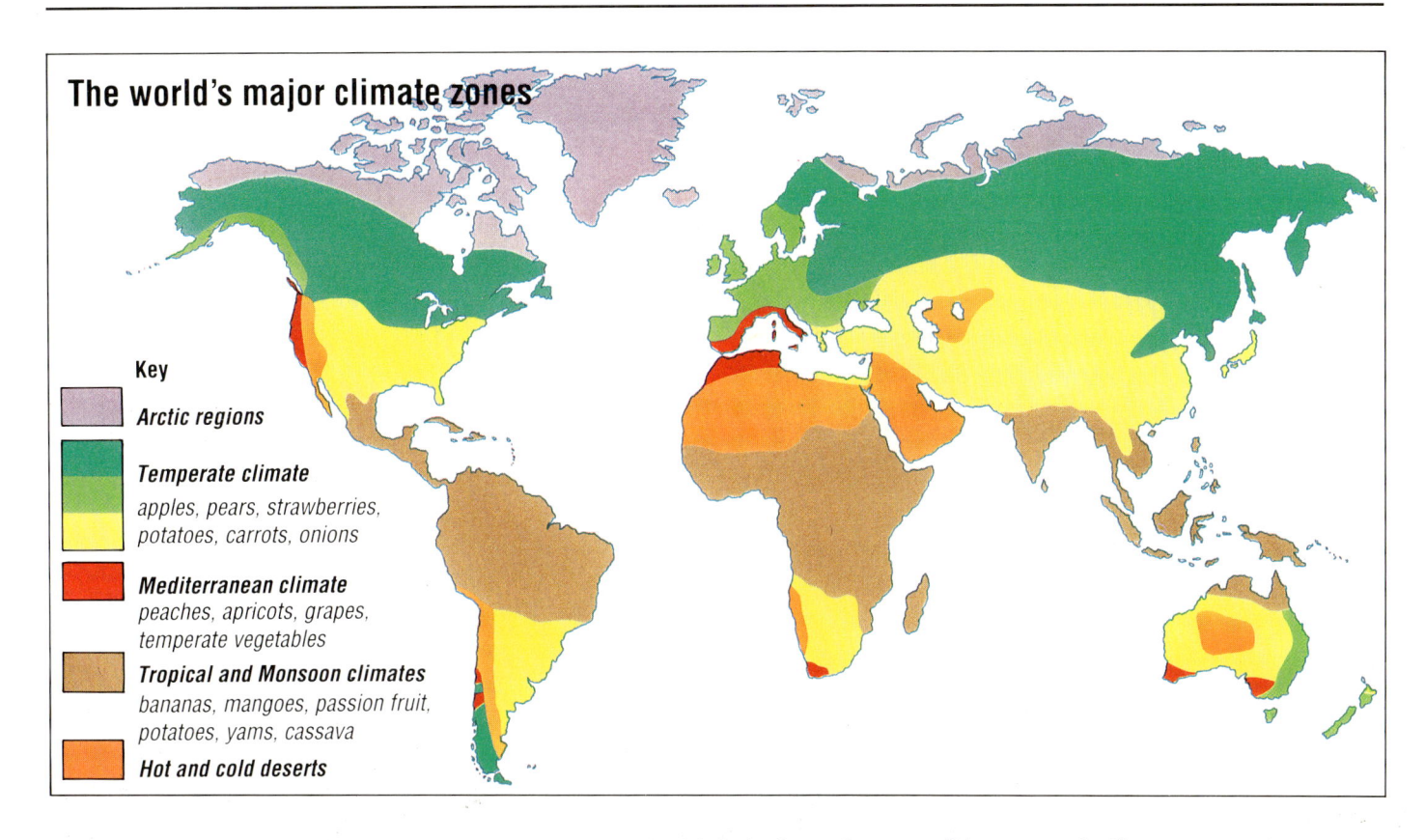

The world's major climate zones

Key
- **Arctic regions**
- **Temperate climate** — apples, pears, strawberries, potatoes, carrots, onions
- **Mediterranean climate** — peaches, apricots, grapes, temperate vegetables
- **Tropical and Monsoon climates** — bananas, mangoes, passion fruit, potatoes, yams, cassava
- **Hot and cold deserts**

The map shows the world's climate zones and which fruit and vegetables grow in them.

In tropical areas the temperature and hours of daylight do not change, so crops can be grown all year round. The warm, moist climate of parts of South America, West Africa and South-east Asia is ideal for growing bananas, mangoes and passion fruit. Important energy-providers like yams, cassava and potatoes are also grown.

In India, Burma and Thailand, rain only falls at certain times of the year. Crop farmers depend heavily upon the monsoon wind that brings rain from June to September.

This banana tree, with its fruit and flower, is on a plantation in New South Wales, Australia.

Luxury crops

Some crops, like coffee, are more valuable for trade than cereal crops, even though we could survive without them. These are called 'luxury' crops. People can make as much money from selling luxury crops as others do from selling oil. Coffee plants need a tropical climate and are grown only in South and Central America, Africa (except for the north) and South-east Asia. However, these countries keep little of the coffee they produce. Most is exported to wealthy places like the USA, Europe and Australia.

Tea is a popular drink all over the world but tea plants can only be grown in the warm, moist areas of India, China, Sri Lanka, Japan and milder parts of the former Soviet Union. For fine-quality teas, only the young shoots are used. They are usually harvested by hand. Coarser leaves are used for lower-quality tea and are harvested by machine.

Chocolate is another luxury food which comes from a tropical crop.

The ripening fruit of a coffee plant. After harvesting, the berries are roasted to give them the typical coffee flavour.

The cocoa plant originated in South America and cocoa is still grown there. However, these days most cocoa is grown in the West African countries of Ghana, Nigeria and Ivory Coast.

Chocolate, tea and coffee are all closely linked with another important crop – sugar. Over half the world's sugar crop comes from sugar cane. This is a giant member of the grass family that grows in moist, tropical areas. Major sugar cane producers include Brazil, Cuba, India, Australia, China and the southern USA. In the cooler climates of Europe, Asia and North America, sugar is produced from a root crop called sugar beet.

Above: *A tea-picker in Zambia, Africa, shows the fresh leaf shoots needed to make fine tea.*

Left: *Selecting newly-harvested cocoa beans in Java, Indonesia.*

Enough for all?

Unfortunately, not all countries can grow crops well. The richer industrial nations sometimes produce too much food, but in poorer countries there are shortages and **famines**. Why?

Some parts of the world are naturally better for growing crops. The temperate climate of North America, Europe, southern New Zealand and parts of Australia provides a regular rainfall and changes in temperature which suit many crops. These countries are also rich from trade overseas. This money is put into developing chemical **fertilizers** to enrich the soil and sprays to kill insects that damage crops. In the last forty years, the industrial countries have produced much more food. In the European Community, the farmers are paid to grow crops. When they produce too much food, the surplus is stored away.

In Europe and the USA, surplus wheat is stored in grain 'mountains'.

Crop-growing is very difficult in places with dry, dusty soil, such as parts of Ethiopia.

In spite of this wealth there are still food shortages in the world. For example in the winter of 1991–2, the former USSR suffered severe food shortages. The harvest did not reach the shops soon enough and so it rotted.

True famines usually happen in tropical areas. In the 1980s famines killed millions of people in Africa, especially in Ethiopia. This area has **droughts** which regularly turn the soil into dust. The dust blows away and leaves the ground useless for farming. Elsewhere there are tropical cyclones which make the rivers flood and also destroy crops. Some places suffer from locust plagues which can devour a harvest in a few hours.

When famines strike in the poorer countries, the richer nations usually send emergency food aid to the starving people. They also loan them money for projects such as irrigation schemes to help them produce food. However, the poor countries find it hard to repay these enormous loans. To raise enough money, countries of Africa and Asia grow **cash crops** like coffee and sugar, which they sell to the richer nations. They grow them on the best land, leaving even less space for food crops to feed their own populations.

The wealthy nations have now started to support projects trying to prevent droughts, such as replanting forests. In the last twenty-five years Ethiopia and other African countries have cleared most of their

A tree nursery in Kenya. Replanting forests is vital in dry areas like this.

A comparison of fertilizer use in different countries

Hundreds of grams per hectare

Countries (left to right): Australia, Brazil, Canada, China, Egypt, Ethiopia, France, India, Malaysia, New Zealand, Philippines, United Kingdom, United States

Scale: 66 to 6219

Source: The Economist Book of World Statistics (1990)

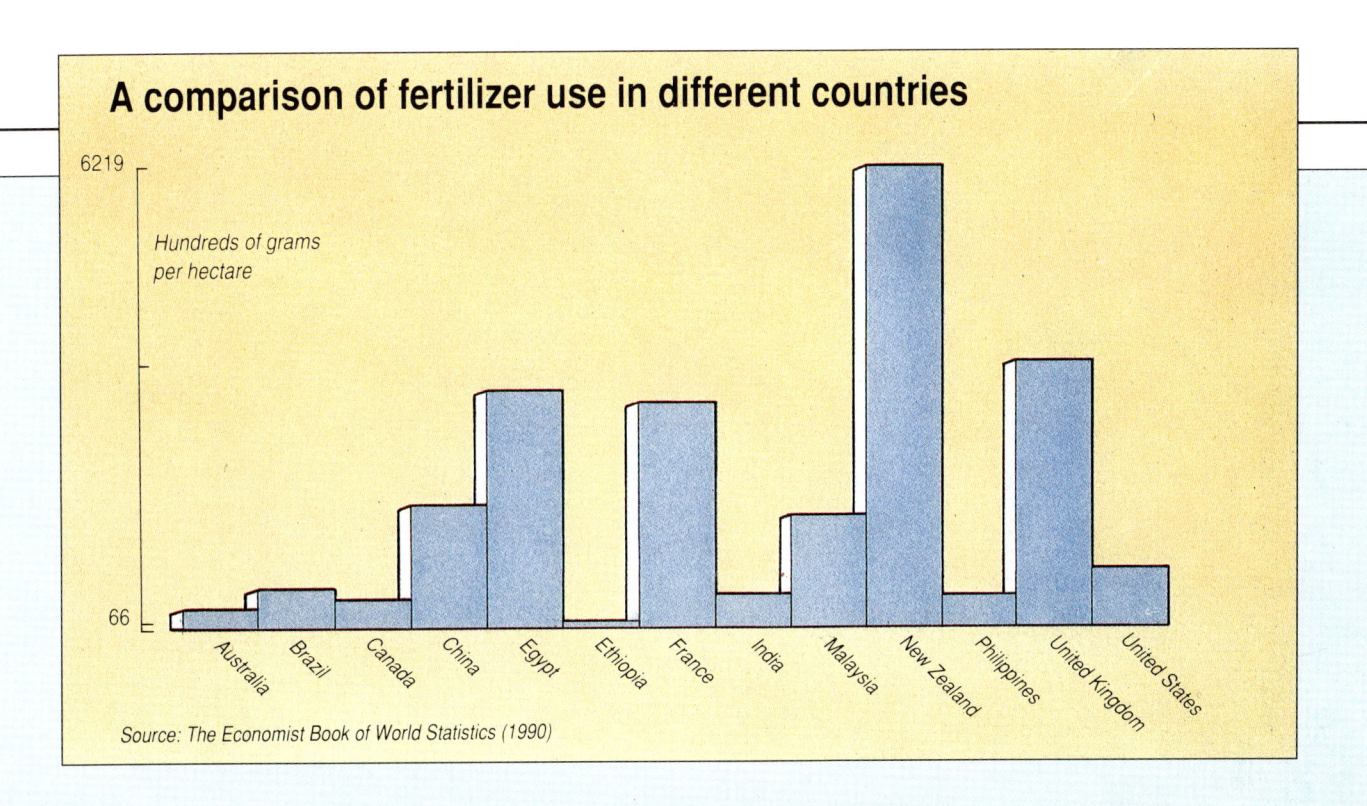

The Green Revolution

In the 1970s farmers in the world's poorer countries tried to grow varieties of wheat and rice which had been developed in industrial countries. This was known as the Green Revolution. The strong new 'supercrops' were supposed to give better **yields** of grain, but they also needed fertilizers and **pesticides** from the industrial countries. The new crops and chemicals proved very expensive and in Asia the pesticides actually led to losses in the yields.

Malaysia, a poor country, uses more fertilizer than industrial Australia.

The problem was that the pesticides did not kill all of Asia's crop pests, but they did kill many pest-eating spiders, beetles and dragonflies which helped to protect the crops. The population of one rice pest, the brown planthopper, increased drastically. During the late 1970s these insects destroyed over 1 000 km^2 of rice fields in South-east Asia. The Green Revolution turned out to be an expensive failure for many people.

forests for farmland. Droughts have become worse and the soil has turned to dust. People hope that the new forests will stop the soil blowing away and will bring more rain. Some of the areas affected by drought now have agricultural colleges. These research into which crops are the most suitable for the region to grow and also show local farmers how they can breed better livestock.

The environment

Every farmer dreams of fertile, flat land for growing crops, but where there are mountains or forests, they must use any available land, good or poor. In Asia, crops are grown successfully in the fertile valleys below the world's highest mountains. However, when farmers clear the trees from the mountain slopes to grow crops, this can cause serious **erosion**. Without the trees to hold it in place, the soil is washed down the slope, leaving it useless for farming.

In the tropics, farmers do not only clear rainforest for cattle grazing.

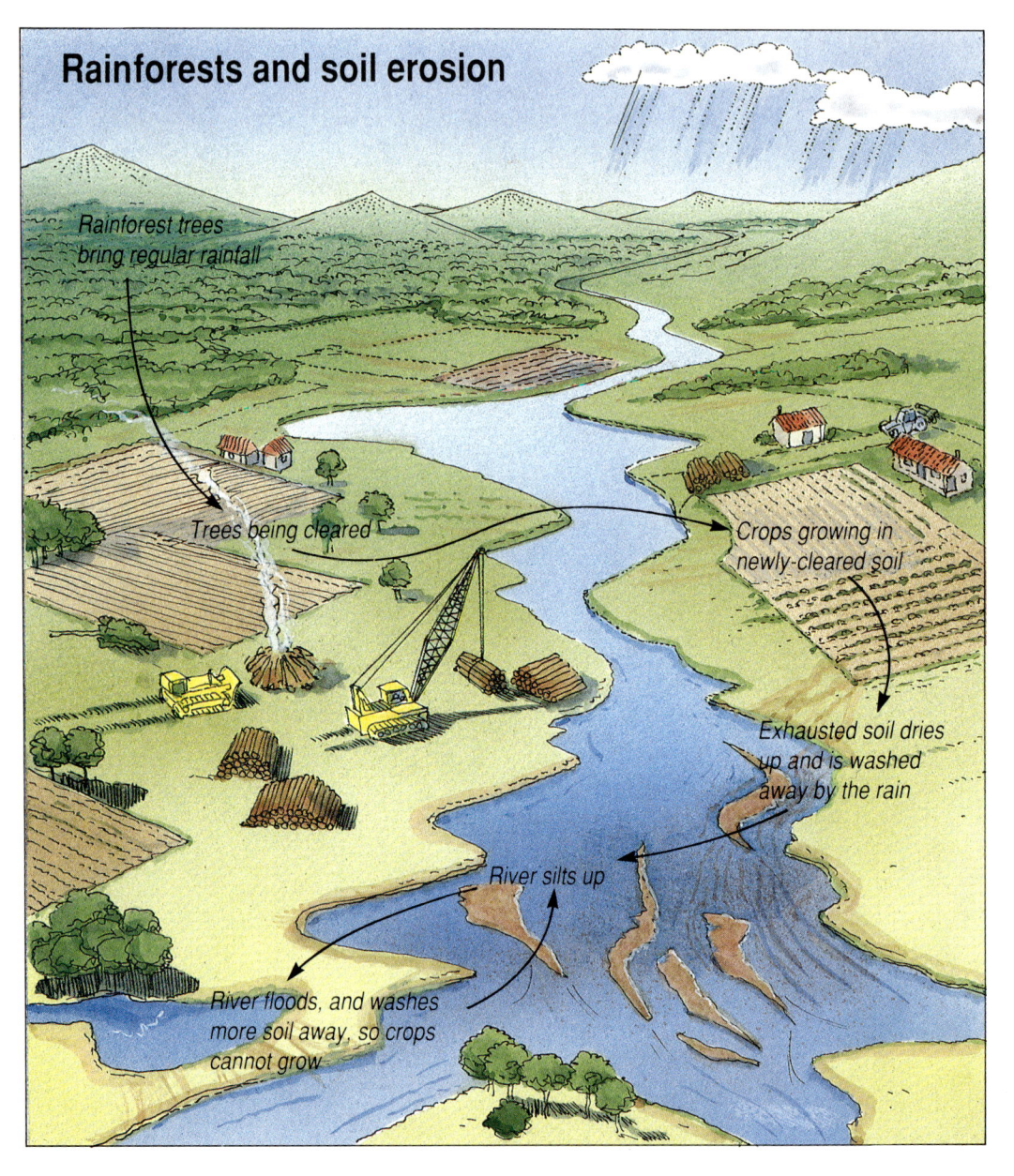

Rainforests and soil erosion

- Rainforest trees bring regular rainfall
- Trees being cleared
- Crops growing in newly-cleared soil
- Exhausted soil dries up and is washed away by the rain
- River silts up
- River floods, and washes more soil away, so crops cannot grow

Left: Clearing forests to make farmland exposes the soil to wind and rain. This can lead to soil erosion.

Right: A stretch of forest cleared for farmland in Sri Lanka. Without the tree cover, the soil soon becomes dry and dusty.

Harvesting the seas

Fish is an important, nutritious food all over the world. Fishing fleets from many nations scour the seas for popular fish such as herring, cod, haddock, Alaska pollock and tuna. The huge nets or harvesting machines catch enormous numbers of fish each time. Such large-scale fishing of some fish, such as herring and cod, is a threat to the survival of the species. This could disrupt the marine **food chain** and could end in the destruction of even more sea life.

Under new laws designed to protect fish stocks, fishermen may only catch a limited number of scarce fish. They must also use nets with larger holes, to allow young fish to escape and breed.

An even better solution is that many countries now farm these scarce fish in tanks or inshore enclosures, instead of harvesting them from the sea.

The fish in this enclosure on a fish farm are now ready to be caught and sold.

People also use vast areas of natural rainforest to grow crops. However, rainforest soil is not suited to agriculture. After a few years the soil is exhausted and new areas have to be cleared for crops. Many people who care for the **environment** are worried that the rainforests, and the wildlife that depends on them for survival, are being wasted in this way. In Cameroon, West Africa, farmers can grow crops in and take timber from some rainforest areas, while other areas are protected in a special national park.

Spraying crops from the air protects them from weeds and pests, but is harmful to wildlife.

Humans need to farm the land but wildlife often suffers. Whenever land is cleared for farming, natural **habitats** are destroyed. Many unusual plants and animals lost their homes when swamps were drained in the Netherlands, the USA and Australia.

The chemical sprays used to control crop pests also harm wildlife. These pesticides do kill harmful insects, but they also kill insects which **pollinate** the crops or eat the pests. If an animal feeds on a poisoned insect, it too is harmed. The poisons can spread from one animal to the next until eventually even large birds of prey may die. **Herbicides** will kill nearby wild flowers as well as weeds.

Fertilizers produce better crops but they also contain chemicals called **nitrates**. Often crops do not take in all these nitrates. Rain washes some off the fields into rivers and lakes, where they **pollute** the water and its delicate wildlife. They can pollute the water we drink too.

Organic farming

These days more farmers are beginning to use **organic** ways of growing plants. To make the soil richer, organic farmers spread crops rich in nitrogen on the land as a green manure. They rotate their crops every few years so that the soil is not exhausted and diseases cannot spread. The sprays they use are often made from plant products. They even use nature's own pest controllers, like ladybirds and hoverfly larvae, to eat aphids. The organic farm products may not be free from blemishes but many people think they are safer to eat, as well as kinder to nature.

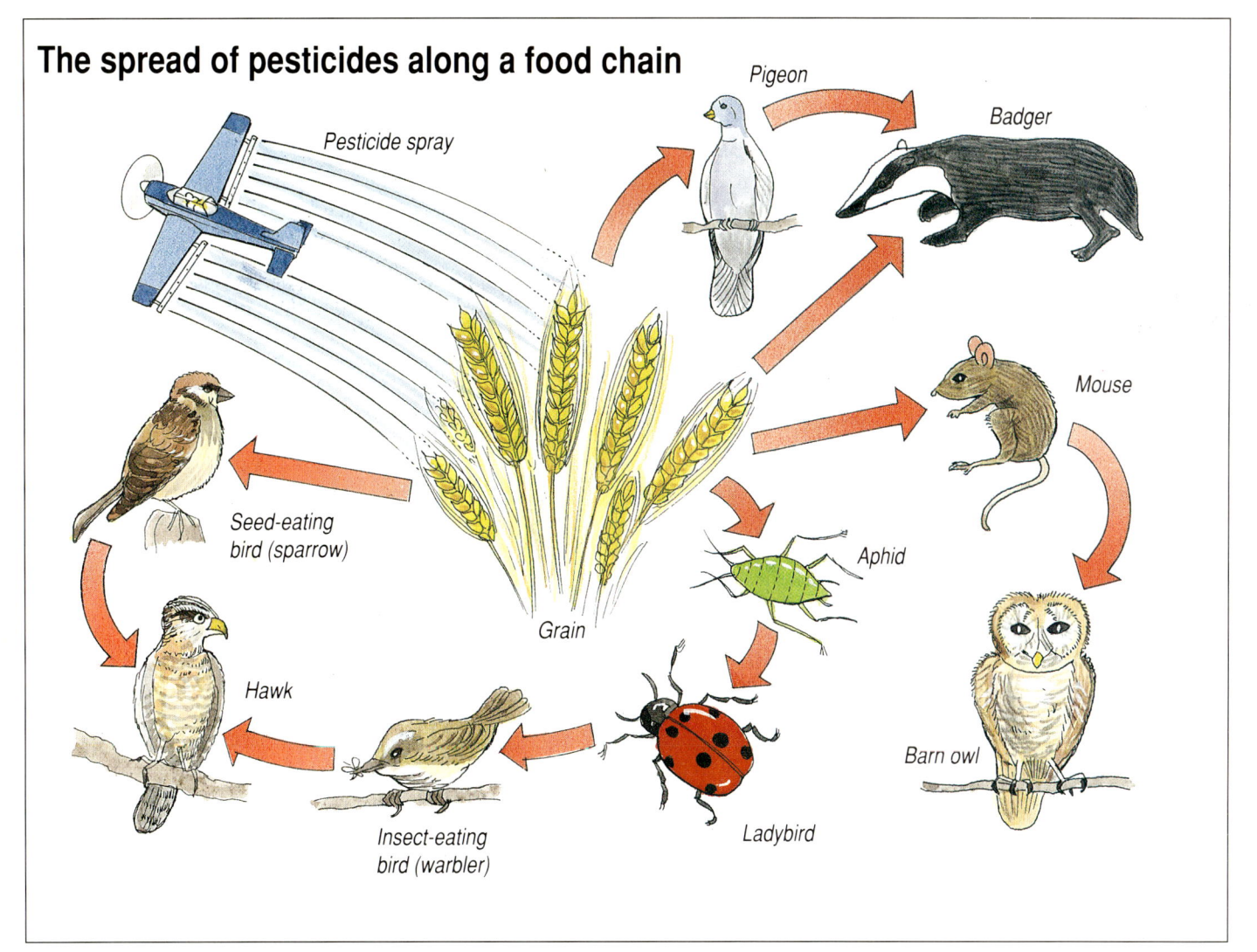

The spread of pesticides along a food chain

The poisons in pesticides can spread through the food chain, harming many animals.

23

How healthy is your food?

Like plant breeders, livestock breeders also want to improve the quality of their products. They now produce meat with less fat, and better quality milk. Farm animals are generally healthier as they are now **vaccinated** against disease and treated with medicines when necessary. However, outbreaks of disease do sometimes occur.

Intensive farms keep great numbers of animals close together. Diseases spread easily. Salmonella is an **organism** that lives in some chickens. It does not harm people who eat the chickens, if the chickens are thoroughly cooked. However, salmonella can cause food poisoning when it is present in eggs, if they are eaten raw or only cooked lightly.

Another disease, BSE, is found mainly in Britain. It affects the brains of cattle. Infected animals behave oddly and have to be destroyed. Outbreaks may be caused by feeding cattle infected meat, instead of their natural diet of grass.

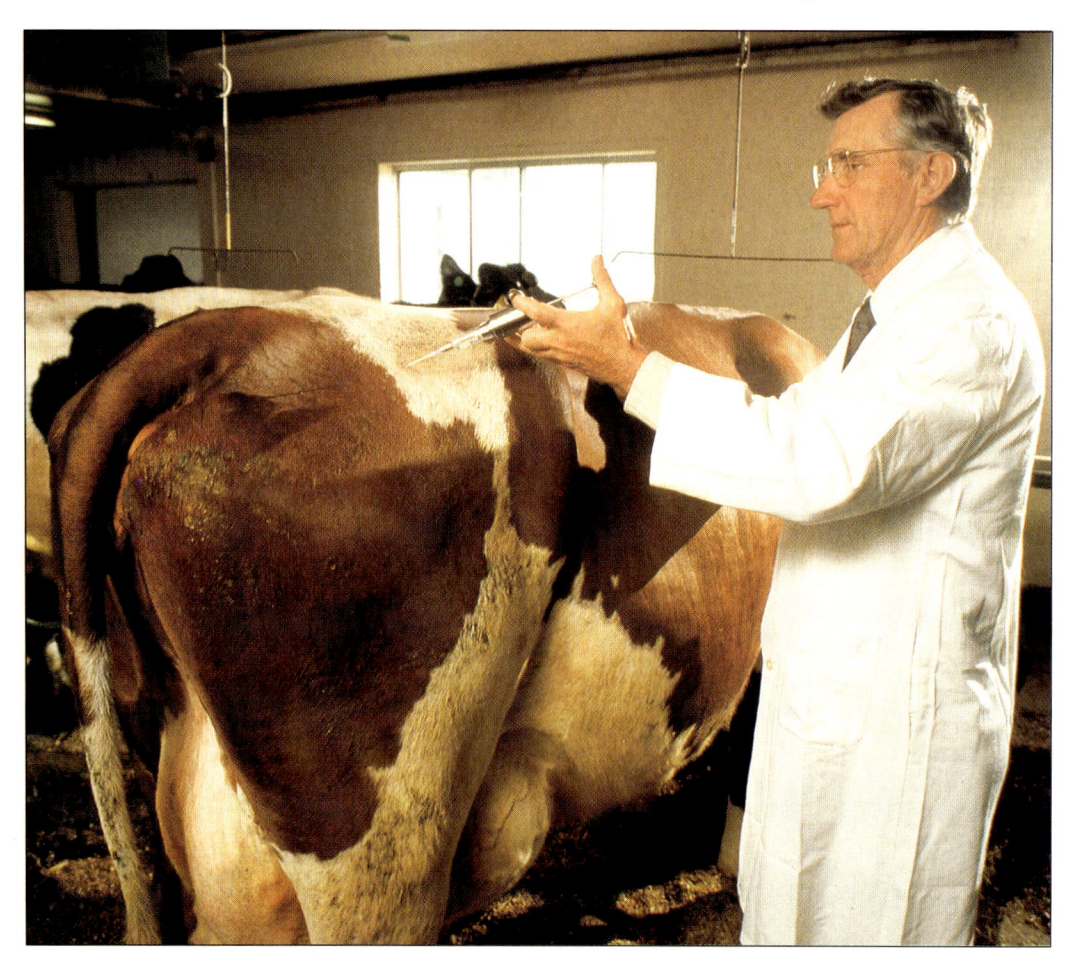

Left: *In wealthier countries, farmers can afford to vaccinate their animals against disease. This is expensive.*

Right: *The eland on this game farm in Zimbabwe are being sprayed to protect them from ticks and other insects.*

Some people now believe that meat is unsafe to eat, especially if it is from intensive farms. Others worry that farm animals are fed too many medicines and fear that some drugs may pass into humans when they eat the meat. In many countries there are strict government regulations to ensure that food is produced safely. However, when you eat or cook a meal, you should always wash your hands first. Keep your kitchen clean and make sure the food is properly cooked.

Disease can spread rapidly among hens kept in cramped conditions.

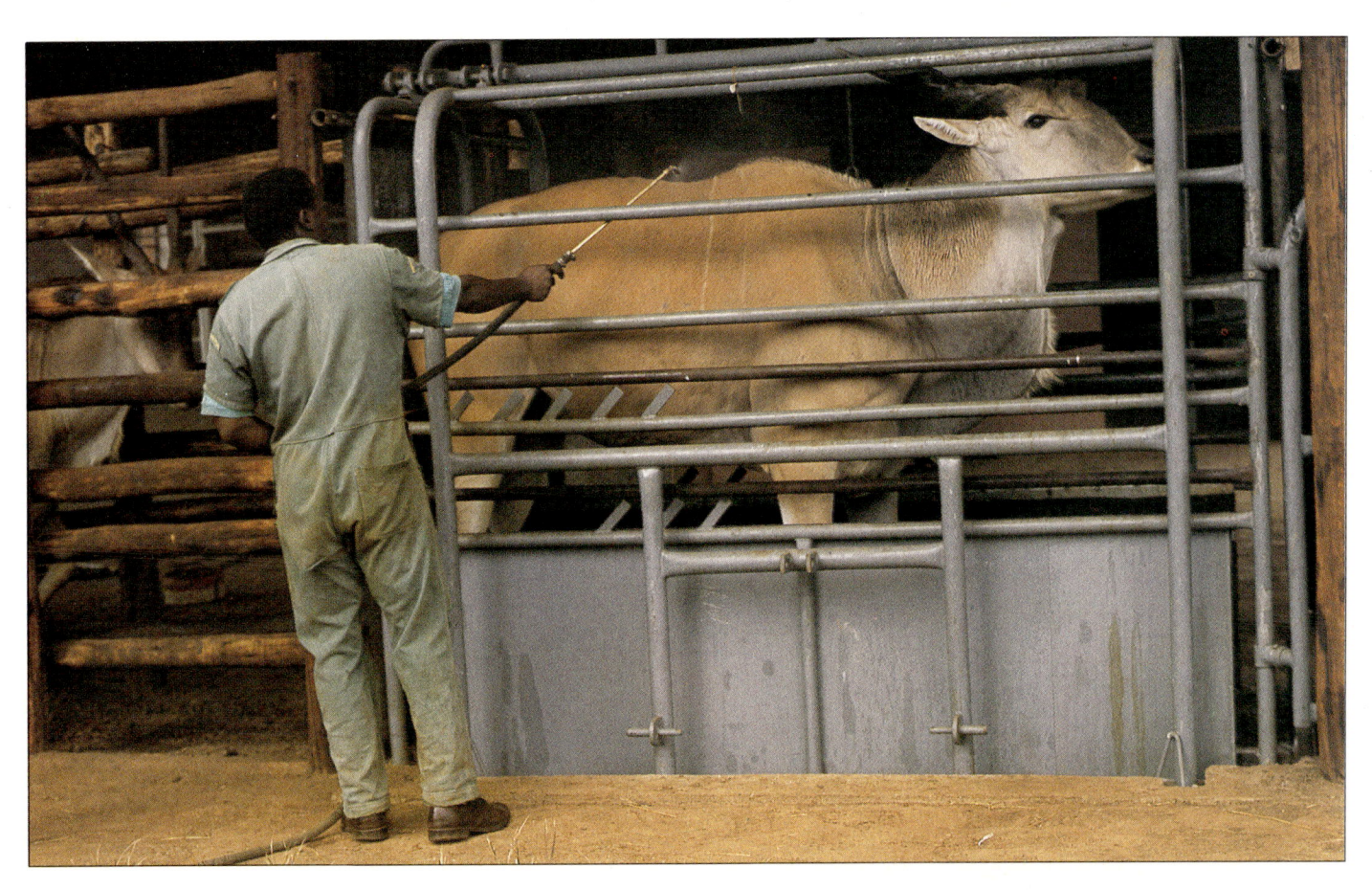

Crops of the future

Thousands of years ago, people chose their seeds from the strongest plants of wild wheat and barley. Ever since, farmers have been trying to improve crop varieties. Today plant breeders are not only trying to improve the yield of a crop or its resistance to disease, they are also creating new plants by changing the **genes** within them. This is called genetic engineering.

Scientists can take a gene with a useful characteristic (like resistance to a particular disease) from one plant and give it to another. For example, a gene that makes a **species** of blackberry thornless could be given to prickly blackberry plants,

Genetic engineering has brought many changes to crop-breeding. Scientists are exploring what plants are made of, in order to create new varieties.

so that they become thornless and easier to pick. Scientists hope to transfer genes from wild grasses that survive in salty soils to different kinds of wheat. Wheat that could grow easily in salty soil would be very useful in tropical countries where the soil is salty from too much irrigation.

Genetic engineering is changing agriculture throughout the world. In India, scientists are testing different kinds of millet to see which grow best in extreme heat. Perhaps one day new crops will be able to survive long droughts, extreme heat and a poor, salty soil. However, we would still need the original wild plants, because they are the only plants that contain the genes needed by scientists for their experiments.

Some people are worried that these important wild crop plants are dying out, as rainforests and other areas are destroyed. For this reason there are now gene banks all over the world, storing the genes and seeds of plants for use in the future.

Above: Over-irrigated soil in hot countries can become salty, as has happened here in Pakistan. Few crops can survive in salty soil.

Right: Seeds, or genes, from thousands of different plants are stored for the future in gene banks.

A changing world

Today farmers can produce much more food than they could forty years ago, thanks to better irrigation, crop breeding and pest control. Even so, we still cannot feed the world. In a few decades there will be millions more people, especially in Africa and Asia. How will they be fed?

To solve this problem, richer countries will have to help poorer ones. Farmers and scientists will have to find new ways of growing crops in difficult conditions. Farming methods will have to change to take better care of the land, wildlife and resources like forests and water. Unless we care for the environment, it will not be able to support us.

The foods we eat and our eating habits are also changing. Over the last fifty years, many people from poorer tropical countries or from eastern Europe have moved to find work in western Europe and North America. They have brought their

Thanks to irrigation, crops can be grown even in hot, parched areas of the desert.

Left: Western-style fast food is popular worldwide. Here people queue for hamburgers in Moscow.

Below: A tourist tries Japanese noodles using traditional chopsticks.

special foods with them. More people are now trying different foods when they go on holiday to faraway places. In this way, diets around the world are changing, as cultures and traditions are mixed.

People are also spending less time cooking, especially in the industrial countries. There is a wide range of **convenience foods** at supermarkets, and people can buy ready-made meals or take-aways. Many people now use microwave ovens to cook foods very quickly.

Do you think you eat different foods from those your parents ate as children? Perhaps in twenty years' time, eating habits and farming methods will be different again from those we know today.

29

Glossary

Cash crops Crops grown in one country purely to be sold to other, richer countries to bring in money.
Convenience foods Foods which need little preparation before they can be eaten.
Drought A long period when not enough rain falls.
Environment All the plants, animals, rocks and rivers around us.
Erosion The wearing-away of rock and soil by wind or water.
Famine A great shortage of food, which causes hunger and starvation.
Fertilizer Something which is added to the soil to make it richer and produce more crops.
Food chain The natural process that makes an animal that feeds on one living thing become food for another.
Genes The tiny units in all living things that pass on characteristics from parents to their offspring.
Habitat The area where a plant or animal lives, such as a meadow or pond.
Herbicides Chemicals designed to kill weeds in crop fields.
Industrial countries Countries which use machinery to build or make things to sell, on a large scale.
Intensive farms Farms which keep large numbers of animals, or grow crops rapidly, to produce high yields. The farmers use chemicals to improve their produce.
Irrigate To bring water to dry land by means of channels, pipes or sprinklers, to help crops grow.

Nitrates Chemicals rich in the nitrogen which plants need to grow.
Organic Natural, or involving plant and animal products. Organic farming only uses fertilizers and pesticides made from animal or vegetable matter.
Organism A living thing, often very tiny.
Pesticide A chemical which kills crop pests.
Pollinate To spread pollen from one plant to another so that it produces seeds.
Pollute To dirty a place with smoke, chemicals or rubbish.
Population The number of people or animals in a place.
Species A group of plants, different from all others.
Staple diet A food that is essential to the diet eaten by people in a particular region.
Technology Scientific research which is directed at helping people to build or make better products.
Temperate regions Parts of the world with a moderate climate which lie between the tropics and polar regions.
Tropical regions The hot parts of the world lying between the Tropic of Cancer and the Tropic of Capricorn.
Tundra Places near the Arctic where the soil underneath the surface is always frozen so that trees cannot grow there.
Vaccinate To give a person or animal a substance that will protect them from a disease.
Yield The amount of food produced from crops or livestock.

Books to read

Baker, S. *Farms* (Macdonald Educational, 1977)
Erlichmann, J. *Poisoned Food?* (Franklin Watts, 1990)
Hadden, S. *Farming* (Wayland, 1991)
Lambert, M. *Food Technology* (Wayland, 1991)
Mountfield, A. *Looking back at Food and Drink* (Macmillan, 1988)
Silvers, D. *In the Kitchen* (Wayland, 1991)
Timberlake, L. *Famine in Africa* (Franklin Watts, 1990)

Picture acknowledgements

The publishers would like to thank the following for allowing their photographs to be reproduced in this book: Bruce Coleman Ltd *front cover* (Gerald Cubitt), 4 (Andy Purcell), 8 (Inigo Everson), 9 below (Dr Eckart Pott), 12 (David Overcash), 13 (Fritz Prenzel), 14 (Eric Crichton), 15 below (Alain Compost), 18 (Mark N. Boulton), 21 below (Dieter & Mary Plage), 25 below (Dr Norman Myers); Eye Ubiquitous 26 (Matthew McKee), 27 above (David Cumming), 29 below (P. M. Field); Tony Stone Worldwide *back cover*, *title page*, 6, 7 below, 10, 15 above, 16, 17, 22, 24, 25 above, 28, 29 above; Wayland Picture Library 9 above; WWF UK (Mauri Rautkari) 21 above. Artwork is by Peter Bull (maps pp. 4–5, 13) and Stephen Wheele.

Notes for activities

Visit a mixed farm if this can be arranged with the farmer, or maybe a smallholding with a few animals. Look out for the different kinds of crops and animals on the farm. You could try to find out why the farmer keeps these particular kinds.

Visit a fruit and vegetable market. Try to find out where the many different fruits and vegetables have come from.

Go around your local shop or supermarket and notice the country of origin of products like flour, sugar, butter, coffee, tea and some tinned foods.

Make a list of some typical meals around the world. Visit a local library and look at books on food and drink to help you. What types of food do your local restaurants have?

Grow some potatoes or tomatoes at school.

Find out which crops are widely grown in your country.

Index

Africa 4, 8, 11, 12–13, 14–15, 17, 18, 21
agricultural colleges 19
Asia 4, 7, 11, 12–13, 14–15, 20, 27
Australia 7, 8, 13, 14–15, 16, 22

BSE 24

Canada 4, 11
cash crops 18, 30
cereal crops 4–5, 10–11, 14, 19, 21, 27
climate 4, 7, 9, 10–11, 12–13, 16
coffee 14–15, 18
convenience foods 29, 30

dairy products 6, 24
diet 6–7, 11, 29, 30
disease 23, 24
droughts 17, 18–19, 30

environment 21, 22, 28, 30
Europe 4, 7, 8, 12, 14–15, 16–17, 22, 28

famines 16–17, 18, 30
farmers 4–5, 19, 20, 26
fertilizers 16, 19, 22, 30
fish 6, 21
food 4, 6–7, 28–9
food chain 21, 22, 30
food poisoning 4

fruit 5, 6–7, 12

genes 26–7
genetic engineering 26–7
government regulations 25
grass 9, 10, 15, 27
Green Revolution 19

harvest 4
hunting 4

India 4, 7, 11, 12–13, 14–15, 27
industrial countries 4, 16, 19, 30
intensive farming 8, 25, 30
irrigation 5, 12, 18, 27, 28, 30

livestock 4–5, 8–9, 10, 19, 20, 24
loans 18
luxury crops 14–15

machines 4, 8, 14
markets 7
meat 8–9, 24–5
medicines 24–5
monsoon wind 13

New Zealand 8–9, 16
nitrates 22, 30
North America 4, 7, 8, 11, 12, 14–15, 16, 22, 28

organic farming 23, 30

pesticides 19, 22, 28, 30
pollution 22, 30
population 4, 11, 28, 30

rainfall 10, 12–13, 16, 19
rainforests 9, 20–1, 27
  replanting of 18–19
rice 7, 11
rivers 5, 22
root crops 12, 15

salmonella 24
seeds 4, 26
soil 4, 9, 21, 23, 27
  erosion of 17, 19, 20, 30
South America 4, 16, 28, 30
sugar 15
supermarkets 7

tea 14–15
technology 4, 16, 28, 30
temperate regions 10–11, 12, 30
temperature 12–13, 16
tropical regions 9, 13, 17, 20, 27, 28, 30

USA 4, 11, 12, 15, 22

vaccination 24, 30
vegetables 6, 12–13

wheat 4–5, 10, 16, 19, 27
wildlife 21, 22, 28